The Complete Guide to FastPass+ and My Disney Experience

Tips & strategies for a magical Disney World vacation

By: Roger Wilk

Copyright Notice
© 2015 Roger Wilk

All rights reserved. This material may not be reproduced, displayed, modified or distributed without the express prior written permission of the copyright holder.

This book is not affiliated in any way with Walt Disney World or the Disney Company.

TABLE OF CONTENTS

1) Introduction — 5

- Why you need this book — 6
- What's in this book anyway? — 9
- Who am I and why should you care? — 12

2) Disney Overview and the History of Disney's FASTPASS® System — 15

- How it all started — 15
- The birth of the FASTPASS® reservation system — 17

3) Introducing FastPass+ — 21

- How FastPass+ works — 22

4) FastPass+ At Each Disney Theme Park — 27

- FastPass+ attractions at Magic Kingdom — 28
- Magic Kingdom FastPass+ kiosks — 31
- FastPass+ attractions at Epcot — 31
- Epcot FastPass+ kiosks — 34
- FastPass+ attractions at Hollywood Studios — 35
- Hollywood Studios FastPass+ kiosks — 36
- FastPass+ attractions at Animal Kingdom — 38
- Animal Kingdom FastPass+ kiosks — 39

5) My Disney Experience & FastPass+ — 41

- Linking Tickets to your Account — 42
- My Disney Experience and FastPass+ — 44
- Modifying your FP+ Selections — 47
- Updating your FP+ Reservations while you're in the Park — 49

What if you've Missed your FP+ Reservation? _____ 49

6) All the Other Things You Can Do With My Disney Experience 51

- My Plans _____ 53
- Attractions _____ 53
- Characters _____ 57
- Dining _____ 58
- Restrooms _____ 60
- Entertainment _____ 61
- Events & Tours _____ 62
- Guest Services _____ 63
- Shopping _____ 64
- Additional My Disney Experience Functionality _____ 65

7) FastPass+ Tips and Tricks 71

8) Let the Magic (and Memories) Begin! 75

Also by Roger Wilk... _____ 78

1) INTRODUCTION

Congratulations! You're going to Disney World! If you've already booked your trip, are in the initial planning stages, or even if you're just curious to find out what Disney World is all about, you've come to the right place. This book will prove to be an invaluable companion to you as you plot and plan your Disney vacation. It will help you make the most of your trip, and provide a huge return on your investment by helping you maximize the time you spend in the parks. By taking all the upfront steps outlined in this book, you'll be planning the perfect Disney vacation so that by the time you get to the parks, you'll arrive with the perfect plan, tailored to the needs of your family.

*The entrance to Magic Kingdom-
The Happiest Place on Earth!*

You'll be miles ahead of the other families who just show up at the gate on their first day at Magic Kingdom or one of the other fantastic theme parks at Walt Disney World, grab a park map on their way in, and try to come to a family consensus on where to go first and what to do next. While they are floundering around near the entrance, or racing down Magic Kingdom's Main Street U.S.A. only to reach the traffic circle at the foot of Cinderella Castle wondering which way to turn, you'll be well on your way to your first FastPass+ reservation as you embark on your fantastic journey. You'll be making magical memories at the Happiest Place on Earth while those that wandered in without a plan are still trying to find their way to Fantasyland.

WHY YOU NEED THIS BOOK

If you've never been to Walt Disney World, or if it's been a few years since your last visit, you may be wondering, "Do I *really* need this book? Can't I just buy my tickets, head to the park and go?" The truth is, you certainly **can** do that! You can visit Walt Disney World without reading this book, or any other Disney travel guide and you'll probably still have a good time. You can easily read the Disney site, or Wikipedia, or do a Google search and find out much of what you need to know- although you may have to do quite a bit of digging in many different places for many of the details you'll find here in this book- all in one place.

If you don't want to do any research at all, you can still hop on a plane and rent a car, or drive to Orlando and pull in to one of the Disney parks, plunk down several hundred of your hard-earned dollars to get your family into a park for the day and walk right in. You can grab a map on the way in and find your way around the parks reasonably well. If you get lost, there will most certainly be a Disney cast member nearby ready to assist. You can walk up to the queue for any attraction that looks interesting, hop in the stand-by line and ride. When you're done with that ride, you can move to the next and the next. Skip the attractions with the really long lines, stop and see a show or two, then at the end of the day head back to your car completely exhausted, and satisfied that you've had a pretty good day.

There are plenty of great viewing spots for the Festival of Fantasy parade- save your FP+ reservations for something else

While there is certainly something to be said for spontaneity, I can assure you with 100% confidence that this is **not** the way to do Disney and promise you that you will **not** be making the most of your time OR your Disney dollars with this approach. Disney is just too expensive, and too crowded to approach in this manner.

You should think of a Disney vacation as an investment and not think of it as a 'get up and go' type of vacation. You'll be investing thousands of dollars in creating the most magical vacation ever, don't you think you should take the time to make it the best vacation possible? Consider the fact that four day park tickets for a family of four will range from around $1,200 for a 'base' ticket, up to more than $1,600 if you upgrade to the Park Hopper and Water Park Fun & More options.

Add in a stay at a Disney resort or other nearby accommodations, airfare, rental car, food, and souvenirs, (which of course you'll need) and depending on the options you choose the total cost of your 'investment' could easily end up in the $3,000-$6,000 range (or more!) Staying for a full week? You could easily be looking at a vacation in the $7,000-$10,000 range! Now you can understand why I think of Disney vacations as 'investments'!

NOTE: If you'd like to find out more about the various Disney ticket options available, or to learn about Disney resorts, parks, and attractions, please check out Discover the Magic: The Ultimate Insider's Guide to Walt Disney World (which also includes an extensive section on Disney vacation planning) or one of my several other Disney travel guides available exclusively on Amazon.com and listed at the end of this book.

WHAT'S IN THIS BOOK ANYWAY?

Each of my Disney guides (this book is my fifth) specializes in a particular facet of the Disney experience. My first title, Discover the Magic (now in its 2nd edition) provides an all-encompassing overview of Walt Disney World and planning a Disney vacation. Disney Tips & Secrets provides nearly 250 tips and secrets to help you save time and money inside the parks of Walt Disney World. Disney Christmas Magic is geared exclusively toward those planning or considering a Disney vacation during the most wonderful time of the year, and Keys to the Kingdom provides everything you need to know about Magic Kingdom- the crown jewel of all the Disney Parks.

Magic Kingdom's Main Street U.S.A.

I have deliberately written my Disney travel guides to be segmented and specialized to allow each reader to pick and choose which ones are right for them. I am of the firm belief that most people don't need (or want) to plod through a 1,500 page encyclopedia-sized travel guide in order to take a vacation. I believe reading a guide like that cover to cover is a daunting task for most- I know I certainly don't want to spend that much time and effort planning **any** vacation. For less than the price of a latte or cappuccino, you can pick up one of my Disney guides and know that your time and money will be well spent.

In this book, I'll begin by providing a brief history of Walt Disney World and Disney's now extinct paper FASTPASS® reservation system. This will provide you a good idea of how we arrived where we are today. Next, you'll learn everything you need to know about Disney's exclusively awesome (and FREE) FastPass+ reservation system. I'll provide the ins and outs of FastPass+ and give you the details on how to use it as you plan your vacation- and equally important when (and when not) to use it while you're in the parks.

This book also contains a complete guide to the My Disney Experience travel planning application, and how you'll absolutely need it as you prepare for your Disney vacation from your desktop computer, tablet, or mobile device. I'll explain all the functions of the app so you'll be prepared to do everything from checking wait times or making dining reservations, to checking the start time of your favorite show or parade or finding out where your favorite characters are at any point in time. I'll also explain how essential the app will be, and how you'll benefit from using the My Disney Experience mobile app **during** your vacation as you travel from park to park. You see, Disney vacation planning doesn't end when your vacation begins. You'll be using FastPass+ and My Disney Experience throughout your magical Walt Disney World adventure as you 'tweak' your vacation on the fly.

Make My Disney Experience an integral part of your Disney vacation

Since My Disney Experience and FastPass+ work together to complement each other very well, in many ways the two sections of this book will overlap. I'll explain how the two can become the perfect travel companions (along with this book of course) as you traverse the miles and miles of magic that is Walt Disney World.

WHO AM I AND WHY SHOULD YOU CARE?

My name is Roger Wilk, and I'm a married father of three residing in the upper Midwest. As you may have guessed by now, I am also a huge, huge Disney fan. I'll never forget my first Disney vacation so many years ago when I walked through the gates of Magic Kingdom and gazed upon Cinderella Castle for the first time. As I walked down Main Street U.S.A., I quickly realized that it's not just marketing hype, Disney truly is the most magical place on earth.

It was back in January of 2012 when I was transformed from a casual Disney fan to an 'all in' die-hard living, breathing Disney fanatic. I had just suffered a major career setback in mid-December, just before the holiday break. I went into the Christmas season feeling pretty miserable and depressed. Thankfully, we had previously booked a Disney vacation and were scheduled to fly to Orlando on January 1st. After landing, we went straight to Magic Kingdom.

As I walked down Main Street U.S.A. that day I felt all my cares and worries about my career simply melt away. Throughout the trip, The Happiest Place on Earth brought me out of the doldrums and truly transformed me into the Disney freak I am today. It was shortly thereafter, in the spring of 2012, that I decided to write a book about my adventures in an effort to share all that I had learned, and to help other families create the magical memories I have had the privilege of sharing with my own family. I had read several Disney travel guides myself and thought, "I can do this!" And so I did. I had no idea if anyone would be interested in what I had to say, but hoped that some would find my point of view informative, entertaining, and valuable in their quest to plan the perfect Disney vacation.

My family of Disney fanatics

Now, several years, tens of thousands of copies and five titles later (eight if you count 2nd editions) I continue to visit Disney and write about my adventures. As the #1 best-selling independent family travel author on all of Amazon.com, I must be doing something right! I'll continue to write as long as you and thousands of other Disney aficionados like you will continue to be interested in all I have to say.

Well, enough about me, let's get to the real reason you're here. It's time to relax and enjoy, and **Let the Memories Begin!**

2) DISNEY OVERVIEW AND THE HISTORY OF DISNEY'S FASTPASS® SYSTEM

HOW IT ALL STARTED

Magic Kingdom- the original Walt Disney World theme park

Walt Disney World in Orlando began quietly as a dream of none other than Walt Disney himself. In an effort to build upon the great successes of Disneyland in Anaheim, which opened in 1955, Walt expressed a desire to build a similar theme park east of the Mississippi. Although Disneyland had become highly successful, one of the challenges Disney faced with the park was the lack of land area for future expansion. He considered this as he began secretly scouting locations in the eastern half of the country for what would eventually be dubbed 'The Florida Project'.

As he scouted locations for the project, Walt wanted to ensure he would have room for more than just one theme park, and that he'd have room for expansion into areas such as scientific and residential development. Once Walt had settled on the central Florida location along the I-4 corridor, the Walt Disney Company created multiple shell corporations with cryptic names such as Reedy Creek Ranch, Inc., Compass East Corporation, and Tomahawk Properties, Inc. so they could acquire the land at reasonable prices. Disney knew that land prices would skyrocket if landowners got wind of his plan. As you stroll down Main Street U.S.A. at Magic Kingdom on your next trip, check out some of the buildings lining the street. You will still see the names of these corporations adorning the windows.

While Disney acquired the land in Florida (47 square miles in all- twice the size of the island of Manhattan), Walt unveiled his Experimental Prototype Community of Tomorrow (EPCOT). This was one of his original plans for the land. Unfortunately, Walt Disney never had the chance to see his dream realized. He died of lung cancer a year before construction of the Magic Kingdom resort and theme park began in 1967. (For more info on Magic Kingdom including a complete ride guide and park maps, check out Keys to the Kingdom.)

The crown jewel of all Disney parks, Magic Kingdom opened on October 1st, 1971 along with the first two hotels of Walt Disney World: Disney's Contemporary Resort and

Disney's Polynesian Resort. The park opened with 23 attractions and six themed 'lands' similar to those of Disneyland in California, with the only unique land being Liberty Square. Since its opening in 1971, Walt Disney World has expanded to include four major theme parks, two giant water parks, the Downtown Disney (soon to be renamed Disney Springs) shopping and entertainment complex and nearly 30 resorts.

Discover the Magic of Cinderella Castle

THE BIRTH OF THE FASTPASS® RESERVATION SYSTEM

As the years since the opening of Magic Kingdom have progressed, the success of Walt Disney World has grown by leaps and bounds. In fact, 4th quarter 2014 attendance was the largest in Disney history, and with annual attendance of over 50 million guests, the four major theme parks of

Walt Disney World occupy four of the top eight amusement park attendance rankings in the world! (Note: The other four of the top eight are Disney parks as well.)

As attendance continued to grow in the 1990s, Walt Disney World became a victim of its own success and needed a plan to handle the huge crowds entering the parks each year. In 1999, with overall park attendance topping the 40 million mark, the Walt Disney Company needed a way to moderate the high wait times at Disney World's most popular attractions and addressed this issue by launching a ride reservation system called FASTPASS®.

Disney's classic paper FASTPASS® system is now a thing of the past

FASTPASS was available for the most popular rides and attractions at all four Disney theme parks. The paper process was fairly simple. Rather than going to the stand-by ride entrance queues, you headed to the area near the entrance where you would find FASTPASS distribution kiosks. You would insert your park ticket into the FASTPASS machine and out would pop your FASTPASS ticket.

A one hour ride window would be printed on the ticket, as would the time that you would be eligible to obtain your next FASTPASS. Instead of waiting in line for an hour or two at the most popular attractions, you would be free to roam around the park and enjoy some of the other attractions until the time of your reservation. Instead of getting into the regular line, you proceeded to the FASTPASS Return line and pretty much walked right on! FASTPASS was a boon for customer service and satisfaction, and always FREE!

Over the years of increasing attendance at all of Disney's parks, the system began to get a bit overwhelmed. As anyone who has ever gone to Hollywood Studios in the afternoon during peak seasons in the hopes of grabbing a Toy Story Midway Mania FASTPASS will attest, it got to the point that the paper system just didn't work anymore. It was then that Disney decided to scrap the paper FASTPASS system and replace it with the all electronic FastPass+ system.

The Twilight Zone Tower of Terror is one of the most popular FastPass+ attractions at Hollywood Studios

3) INTRODUCING FASTPASS+

FastPass+ is the next step in the evolution of Disney's ride reservation system, and takes the original paper system to an entirely new level. The paper FASTPASS distribution kiosks situated at the ride queues of the most popular park attractions have been replaced by a limited number of walk-up electronic kiosks at each park, and the new My Disney Experience planner and mobile app. Rather than obtaining your ride reservation at the attraction while inside the parks, FastPass+ allows you to reserve your attractions up to 30 days prior to your Disney vacation of you're staying offsite, and up to 60 days in advance if you're staying at a resort on Disney property. If you are visiting Disney as a day guest (purchasing your tickets at the gate) you will only be able to make your reservations at the kiosks after you've entered the park.

NOTE: As you read through this chapter on FastPass+ and the chapter on My Disney Experience, you'll notice some overlap between the content of the two chapters. FastPass+ and My Disney Experience are designed to complement each other. You certainly can't have one without the other. In this chapter, I'll focus on a general overview of FastPass+ and how it works. I'll keep the My Disney Experience references limited to the app as it applies to FastPass+. In the My Disney Experience chapter, I'll go into more detail on booking and updating your fast passes using My Disney Experience, and on all of the other great features of the app above and beyond using it for FastPass+ reservations.

HOW FASTPASS+ WORKS

When you purchase your Disney tickets, you simply link them to your account so you can choose your FastPass+ attractions. The sooner you do this, the better. (You'll find complete instructions for registering your My Disney Experience account and linking your tickets in Chapter 5 – My Disney Experience and FastPass+.) As your trip gets closer than 60 days (if you're staying onsite) or 30 days (if you're staying off property) the longer you wait, the bigger chance you won't get the FastPass+ reservations you're hoping for. Some of the most popular attractions like Seven Dwarfs Mine Train at Magic Kingdom, or Soarin' at Epcot are first choices of many when making their reservations. If you don't make yours early, you may be left out in the cold.

When you login to the My Disney Experience app or to your account from the Disney site, you'll be able to pick up to three FastPass+ attractions per day at a single park. While this gives you the advantage of being able to plan your day in advance, it can also present challenges because it requires a lot of pre-planning and forethought in order to make the best use of your reservations. You'll need to decide which park you plan to attend on each day of your trip, and if you plan to move from one park to another on the same day, you'll need to decide which of the two parks would be the best use of the three FastPass+ reservations you're allotted in advance each day. If you're also making dining reservations using the My Disney Experience, or by phone, you'll need to make sure you'll be available to ride at the time of your reservation. Nothing is worse than losing track of time while dining with Winnie the Pooh and Friends at The Crystal Palace at Magic Kingdom only to realize your Seven Dwarfs Mine Train reservation has just expired.

Some people don't enjoy being forced to plan their day that far in advance, and some don't even want to be forced to plan things even after they're in the park. Still, it's in your best interest to make an educated guess as to where you'll be and when, so you don't miss out. The good thing is that Disney understands that 'things happen', and you won't be penalized for missing a reservation. Also, if you want to change your plans you can do so at any time, including the same day. Using the free My Disney Experience smart phone app, or one of the FastPass+ kiosks inside each of the parks, you can even change your attractions right up to the minute you're supposed to ride!

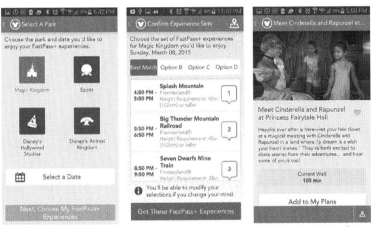

My Disney Experience makes it easy to reserve and modify your FastPass+ reservations

One of the early criticisms that Disney faced after launching FastPass+ in pilot mode in late 2013, and later with the full launch in 2014, was the fact that they limited park guests to three FastPass+ attractions per visitor per day, and they all had to be at a single park. After all, if you played the old paper system correctly, you could get 8-10 passes in a single day at any number of parks. How was this an improvement? Furthermore, the limitation of the new system to only allow guests to reserve their FastPass+ attractions at a single park greatly reduced the benefits of the Park Hopper add-on to the standard Magic Your Way ticket option. As Disney worked out the kinks in the system they tweaked it to give all park guests a better experience.

Some 'meet and greets' are very popular with the kids!

Although you are still limited to three advance reservations per day, and they are still required to be at a single park, you are now able to add additional reservations after your initial passes are used (or have expired) by visiting the kiosks within the parks. Also, if you have the Park Hopper option, you can use your pre-reserved passes at one park then hop over to another to visit a kiosk at the new park to reserve your next pass. Once you've used that pass, you can again visit a kiosk to reserve another (and so on, and so on...) A great FastPass+ strategy for those with the Park Hopper option is to get all of your passes at the first park as early in the day as possible so you're able to hop over to the 2nd park earlier in order to make as many additional reservations as possible before the park closes.

FastPass+ was made for rides like Toy Story Midway Mania

Of course, as with the old system the success of leveraging this system is still subject to availability of the passes at the 2nd park. Don't expect to travel to Disney during peak seasons and use your passes at Magic Kingdom for example, then hop on over to Epcot in the afternoon to grab a Soarin' reservation and then hop to Hollywood Studios in the evening and be able to grab a Toy Story Midway Mania or Rock n Roller Coaster FastPass+ reservation. It's not going to happen. Still, it's a decent strategy and a nice feature to be able to have the flexibility to at least try it!

The Seven Dwarfs Mine Train has the longest wait times at Magic Kingdom

4) FASTPASS+ AT EACH DISNEY THEME PARK

Each of the four theme parks at Walt Disney World has several attractions and activities available for FastPass+ reservations. The reservations are not limited to just the rides at each of the parks. You can also make FastPass+ reservations for a variety of 'meet and greets' such as meeting Anna and Elsa from Frozen at Magic Kingdom's Princess Fairytale Hall, or Mickey Mouse at the Town Square Theater (also at Magic Kingdom). You can also use your three FastPass+ reservations to reserve premium seating at some of Walt Disney World's most popular parades and shows such as the Festival of Fantasy afternoon parade at Magic Kingdom, or IllumiNations at Epcot.

NOTE ABOUT FP+ Ratings: In this section, I'll give each FastPass+ attraction a rating based somewhat on the quality of the attraction (5 Mickeys is high, 1 is low), but more so based on an attractions worthiness of being one of your cherished three FP+ reservations. There are many great attractions that are simply not in high enough demand to warrant using one of your reservations, so they will have a low FastPass+ rating. There are also many great parades and shows that have plenty of seating or viewing available, so you won't need a FP+ reservation for those either. This does not mean you should not check them out if they interest you! It simply means that either the lines are not super long (most of the day) or there is plenty of seating available, so you'd be better off saving your reservations for something else.

FASTPASS+ ATTRACTIONS AT MAGIC KINGDOM

Magic Kingdom is the crown jewel of all Disney parks, and is likely the place where you'll spend much of your time during your Disney vacation. It is also the most crowded Disney park and (thankfully) the park with the most FastPass+ attractions.

Splash Mountain and Space Mountain are very popular attractions at Magic Kingdom

Here are a few notes and things to consider about some of the FastPass+ attractions at Magic Kingdom... Big Thunder Mountain Railroad (BTMR) and Space Mountain are both moderately intense coasters, although not nearly to the level of Rock n Roller Coaster at Hollywood Studios, or that of Expedition Everest at Animal Kingdom. Most kids who meet the height requirement of BTMR will enjoy the ride. Although it features quite a few dips and twists, it should be pretty fun for most. Space Mountain might be a little 'iffy' for the younger set, or for those with back or neck trouble. The entire ride takes place in the dark, and you're sure to be jolted back and forth throughout your journey into space. Consider that before devoting one of your FastPass+ reservations to this attraction.

You can use a FP+ reservation to meet talking Mickey at the Town Square Theater

As you read through the ratings for each park, you'll notice the 'meet and greet' attractions are rated pretty low. One exception to this is the opportunity to meet Anna and Elsa at Princess Fairytale all in Magic Kingdom's Fantasyland. There is frequently a very long line to meet these two sisters, so if your little princess would like to meet them, it may be well worth your investment in a FastPass+ reservation for this meet and greet. On the next page is a look at the FastPass+ attractions at Magic Kingdom.

Attraction	Description	FP+ Rating
Ariel's Grotto	Meet the star of The Little Mermaid	🐭
The Barnstormer	Mini-coaster with thrills for tiny tikes	🐭🐭
Big Thunder Mountain Railroad	Mine train coaster- "the wildest ride in the wilderness!"	🐭🐭🐭🐭🐭
Buzz Lightyear's Space Ranger Spin	Blast Zurg and save the galaxy in this intergalactic romp	🐭🐭🐭
Dumbo the Flying Elephant	Go round and round on a flying elephant	🐭🐭
Enchanted Tales with Belle	An interactive play with Belle	🐭🐭🐭
Festival of Fantasy	Disney's awesome afternoon parade	🐭
The Haunted Mansion	Board your 'doom-mobile' for a haunted and hilarious romp	🐭🐭🐭
it's a small world	Here this catchy tune in multiple languages while traveling the globe	🐭
Jungle Cruise	Set sail for high adventure	🐭🐭
Mad Tea Party	Take a spin on Disney's classic teacups	🐭
The Magic Carpets of Aladdin	Fly high over Agrabah	🐭🐭
Main Street Electrical Parade (evening parade)	Catch the sights and sounds of Disney's evening parade	🐭
The Many Adventures of Winnie the Pooh	Tour the Hundred Acre Wood in your oversized Hunny Pot	🐭🐭🐭
Mickey's PhilharMagic	Get swept away in magical Disney animation	🐭🐭
Monsters, Inc. Laugh Floor	Giggle to a live comedy show starring hilarious stars from the movies	🐭
Peter Pan's Flight	Journey over London to Never Land	🐭🐭
Pirates of the Caribbean	A swashbuckling adventure with Captain Jack Sparrow	🐭🐭🐭
Princess Fairytale Hall: Meet Cinderella	Meet and greet Cinderella	🐭
Princess Fairytale Hall: Meet Anna and Elsa from Frozen	Meet the stars of Disney's instant classic	🐭🐭🐭
Seven Dwarfs Mine Train	An adventurous family coaster	🐭🐭🐭🐭🐭
Space Mountain	Blast off through outer space	🐭🐭🐭🐭🐭
Splash Mountain	A twisting, turning log flume ride through Disney's "Song of the South"	🐭🐭🐭🐭🐭
Tomorrowland Speedway	Put the pedal to the metal on this scenic motorway	🐭🐭
Town Square Theater Mickey Mouse Meet and Greet	Meet the only talking Mickey at Disney	🐭
Under the Sea: Journey of the Little Mermaid	Descend beneath the waves in the splashy musical adventure	🐭🐭
Wishes Nighttime Spectacular	A magical end to a magical day	🐭

MAGIC KINGDOM FASTPASS+ KIOSKS

There are several locations in Magic Kingdom where you can stop by a FastPass+ kiosk to reserve additional passes after you've exhausted your original three. They are:

1. Mickey's PhilharMagic in Fantasyland
2. Diamond Horseshoe in Liberty Square
3. Jungle Cruise in Adventureland
4. Stitch's Great Escape in Tomorrowland

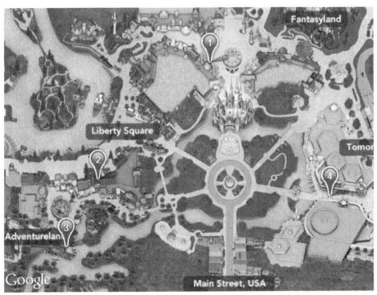

Locations of FP+ kiosks at Magic Kingdom

FASTPASS+ ATTRACTIONS AT EPCOT

Because of the limited number of overall attractions at Epcot, the list of FastPass+ attractions is much shorter than that of Disney's Magic Kingdom. Due to the limited number of high demand attractions at Epcot, you must pick your attractions from two different 'tiers' or groups of attractions. You are able to choose one attraction from Group A, and two attractions from Group B. Although you'll find this to be a bit frustrating, it's a necessary step that Disney must take. Otherwise everyone would pick Soarin' and Test Track the two most popular attractions at Epcot, and two of the most popular in all of Walt Disney World, and few would choose anything else.

FP+ is essential at Soarin' and Test Track, but since they're both in the same group, which will you choose?

Below is a list of FastPass+ attractions at Epcot and their ratings. As I mentioned in the previous section, please remember that the FastPass+ rating is not to be confused with an overall rating for the attraction. For example, although Epcot's awesome IllumiNations closing show is definitely a 'must see' attraction, it has a very low FP+ rating because it can be seen very well from anywhere around the International Lagoon. Premium seating provided by the FP+ reservation really isn't needed. You will also note that although Test Track and Soarin' are both awesome attractions, I'm giving Soarin' a slightly lower FP+ rating. The rationale for this is that the wait times for Soarin' tend to be a bit shorter than those of Test Track, and also there are fun activities to play while you wait in the queue that make the time pass more quickly. Keep in mind- you get to choose one from Group A and two from Group B.

Attraction	Description	FP+ Rating
Group 'A' attractions (Pick 1):		
IllumiNations: Reflections of Earth	Enjoy the sights and sounds of Epcot's awesome closing show	♥
Soarin'	Feel the wind in your hair as you soar above California	♥♥♥♥♥
Test Track	Design and ride your own concept vehicle in this high-speed thriller	♥♥♥♥♥
Living with the Land	Sail through greenhouses of The Land	♥
Group 'B' attractions (Pick 2)		
Captain EO	Join Michael Jackson and his crew as they try to save the universe	♥
Journey Into Imagination With Figment	Join the playful purple dragon on a tour of the Imagination Institute	♥
Mission: SPACE Green	The 'light' version of a NASA-styled space shuttle simulation	♥♥
Mission: SPACE Orange	The full version of the NASA-style mission- not for the faint at heart	♥♥♥
Spaceship Earth	Explore the history of communications from the Stone Age to the future	♥
The Seas with Nemo & Friends	Frolic under the seas with Nemo and his colorful cast of friends	♥
Turtle Talk with Crush	Hang ten for a Q&A session with this totally tubular turtle	♥
Epcot Character Spot	Meet and Greet some of your favorite Disney friends	♥♥

EPCOT FASTPASS+ KIOSKS

After you've used your initial FastPass+ selections, or after the window has expired on your last reservation, stop by one of the kiosks at Epcot to reserve additional attractions. Here are the locations for the FastPass+ attractions at Disney's Epcot theme park:

1. Innoventions West Breezeway
2. Innoventions Plaza Tip Board
3. International Gateway
4. Innoventions East Breezeway

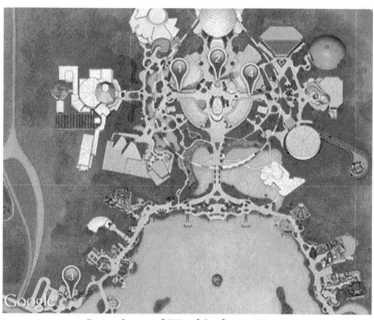

Locations of FP+ kiosks at Epcot

FASTPASS+ ATTRACTIONS AT HOLLYWOOD STUDIOS

Like the FastPass+ arrangement at Epcot, Disney's Hollywood Studios does not have enough high demand attractions to allow you to choose any three you'd like. As with Epcot, the attractions are separated into two groups. You get to choose one attraction from Group A and two attractions from Group B in the chart below.

Attraction	Description	FP+ Rating
Group 'A' attractions (Pick 1):		
Beauty and the Beast - Live on Stage	Get swept away by the romance of this Broadway-style production	🐭
Fantasmic!	See if Mickey can save the day in this breathtaking pyrotechnics show	🐭🐭🐭
Rock 'n' Roller Coaster	Rock on in your super-stretch limo through the freeways of Los Angeles	🐭🐭🐭🐭🐭
Toy Story Mania!	Blast moving targets in this 4D midway-style shooting gallery	🐭🐭🐭🐭🐭
The Great Movie Ride	A star-studded journey through some of Hollywood's most famous films	🐭
Group 'B' attractions (Pick 2)		
Disney Junior - Live on Stage!	Preschoolers' sing, dance, and play	🐭
Indiana Jones Epic Stunt Spectacular!	Cheer on Indy and Marion as they perform stunts from the movies	🐭
Lights, Motors, Action! Extreme Stunt Show	Amazing high-octane stunts	🐭
Muppet*Vision 3D	Hilarious 3D movie with live-action sequences too	🐭
For the First Time in Forever – A Frozen Sing-Along Celebration	Join Anna and Elsa in Arendelle for a fun and frosty interactive showcase	🐭🐭
Star Tours: The Adventures Continue	Feel the Force on this 3D simulated flight into the Star Wars universe	🐭🐭🐭🐭
The Twilight Zone Tower of Terror	This haunted trip to the Hollywood Hotel has its ups and downs	🐭🐭🐭🐭🐭
Voyage of the Little Mermaid	Enjoy the music and highlights from Disney's animated classic	🐭

Due to huge crowds, Fantasmic may be worthy of FP+, but there's always plenty of seating available for Beauty and the Beast

HOLLYWOOD STUDIOS FASTPASS+ KIOSKS

After you've used your initial FastPass+ selections, or after the window has expired on your last reservation, stop by one of the kiosks at Epcot to reserve additional attractions. Here are the locations for the FastPass+ attractions at Disney's Epcot theme park:

1. Corner of Hollywood Boulevard and Sunset Boulevard

2. Sunset Boulevard

3. Toy Story Mania

4. Muppet*Vision 3D

Locations of FP+ kiosks at Hollywood Studios

Rock 'n' Roller Coaster and Toy Story Mania are two of the most popular attractions at Hollywood Studios

FASTPASS+ ATTRACTIONS AT ANIMAL KINGDOM

With attractions such as Kilimanjaro Safaris and Finding Nemo – The Musical, Disney's Animal Kingdom is about much more than just 'the rides'. Therefore the list of FastPass+ attractions is the shortest of any of the parks at Walt Disney World. Since many of those attractions are movies or shows, which will pretty much always have a lower FP+ rating than the rides, the list of high-demand attractions requiring the use of a FastPass+ reservation is pretty short.

Even outstanding shows like Finding Nemo have plenty of seating- save your FP+ for attractions with long wait times instead

When you review the list below, there are a couple of things you should keep in mind. Expedition Everest is arguably the highest intensity true 'thrill coaster' in all of Walt Disney World (with Hollywood Studios' Rock n Roller Coaster running a close second). Therefore, it may be too intense for some members of your family. DINOSAUR is a rough and bumpy ride, but not nearly as intense as 'Everest- however, it is VERY LOUD! Again, this may be one you'll wish to take a 'pass' on if that's not your thing.

Kali River Rapids and Expedition Everest are definitely worthy of your FP+ reservations

ANIMAL KINGDOM FASTPASS+ KIOSKS

Here are the locations for the FastPass+ attractions at Disney's Animal Kingdom theme park:

1. Disney Outfitters
2. Across from the Yak & Yeti Restaurant

3. Island Mercantile

4. Next to Tusker House Restaurant

Attraction	Description	FP+ Rating
DINOSAUR	A very loud and scary prehistoric tour to save a dinosaur from extinction	●●●
Expedition Everest	Thrill coaster set in the Himalayas. Beware of the Yeti!	●●●●●
Festival of the Lion King	Enjoy the pageantry of this Broadway-style show with Simba and friends	●
Finding Nemo - The Musical	Enjoy spectacular music and special effects you must "sea" to believe!	●
It's Tough to Be a Bug!	3D film and live show based on the Disney*Pixar film, A Bug's Life	●
Kali River Rapids	A rip-roaring raft ride through the lush tropical landscapes of Animal Kingdom	●●●●
Kilimanjaro Safaris	Ride an open air cruiser on a tour of the African savanna	●●●●
Meet Favorite Disney Pals at Adventurers Outpost	Meet Safari Mickey & Minnie at their exploration headquarters	●
Primeval Whirl	Spin through a maze of curves and dips on this twisting coaster	●

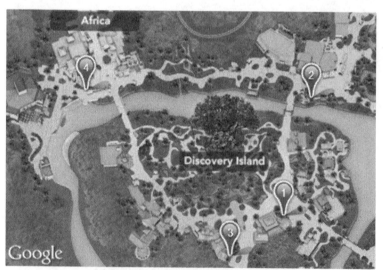

Locations of FP+ kiosks at Animal Kingdom

5) MY DISNEY EXPERIENCE & FASTPASS+

Although Disney's new FastPass+ reservation system could certainly exist without My Disney Experience, it would not be nearly as effective without its partnering app. Just as the old paper FASTPASS® system existed in Disney parks prior to the rollout of FastPass+ in 2013, the new system could function to some degree without the app.

The My Disney Experience mobile app

Of course, many of the features of FP+ could not exist without My Disney Experience. It would be impossible to reserve your attractions 60 days in advance (30 days if you're staying offsite) without the My Disney Experience app. It would be much more difficult to modify your selections prior to your visit, or modify them after you've entered a park for the day without My Disney Experience. Sure you could use the kiosks for all of your initial reservations and updates, but then it wouldn't be much of an improvement over the old system which had the equivalent of a kiosk at each FASTPASS attraction. Yes- it certainly would be much more difficult to plan and enjoy your vacation without the benefits afforded by My Disney Experience.

My Disney Experience is available via a desktop site by registering your email address and logging in at MyDisneyExperience.com. You can also download the free app for your mobile phone or tablet. The true beauty of the app is the fact that not only does it allow you to manage your FP+ reservations, it does SO MUCH MORE! On your next Disney vacation, you'll use the app for tons of research and planning tasks you'll need to complete to make the most of your trip. You'll research all the attractions, check their wait times, make dining reservations, check on show and event times, find characters, and do all the other little things to make your Disney vacation as magical as it can be. To make the most of it, you'll want to learn the ins and outs of the app, and learn about all the little things it can do to help. By reading this book, you'll already be miles ahead of the other 'non planners' as you make your way to the parks.

LINKING TICKETS TO YOUR ACCOUNT

When your tickets arrive, the first thing you'll want to do is link them to your My Disney Experience account. You can do this in all versions of the app (mobile, tablet, desktop). To do this, simply navigate to the Reservations menu in the app and select Link Tickets in the Tickets and Passes section. From this point there are two ways to complete the process. You can simply enter the 12 digit number on the back of the ticket, or you can scan the QR code on the back of the ticket. Next, select the guest you wish to associate with that ticket, and you're done! It's that simple.

Link your tickets by scanning the QR code or entering the ID number

Now that we have the busy work out of the way, let's get down to business and talk about how you'll use My Disney Experience to manage your FastPass+ reservations.

Note about screen shots in this book: Throughout this section you'll find samples of many screen shots of My Disney Experience. Some will be from the desktop version, some from the Android mobile version, and some from the iPad version. Depending on the device (or browser) you're using, the screen you see may not look exactly like the screen samples in this book. Also, Disney periodically updates both the mobile and desktop apps, so you may notice slight changes in appearance and functionality.

MY DISNEY EXPERIENCE AND FASTPASS+

After you've made your Disney resort reservations (if you're staying on-property) and purchased your park tickets, your next step is to install the My Disney Experience app to your mobile device so you can register your tickets and link them to your reservation. You can also purchase your tickets directly through the app if you prefer. (More on that later.)

After you install the app, you'll need to login using your email and password. If you already have an account through Disney (which you may have if you booked your hotel reservation online, or if this is not your first trip) you'll use the same email and password. If not, you'll need to register by clicking the 'Create Disney Account' link before you'll have complete access to the app.

After you've logged into the mobile app, or the desktop site, you'll see a summary screen similar to the samples below. It will provide details of the plans you've booked so far- so if you've booked dining reservations over the phone, they should already be linked to your account. If you're using the desktop app, you can hover over the My Disney Experience option on the menu bar. If you're using the mobile app, simply tap the three lines or Mickey icon in the upper left-hand corner of the screen, and you'll see a menu similar to the samples below. You'll notice the options and their order vary depending on which version you're using. I'll cover each option in detail, but for now, let's talk FastPass+.

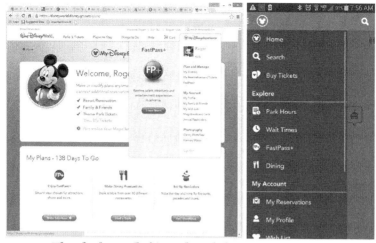

*The desktop (left) and mobile versions of the
My Disney Experience welcome screen*

Since you haven't made any FP+ reservations yet, we'll add some next. Later, I'll show you how to modify the reservations which can be done using both the desktop and mobile versions of the app. First, select a day for your reservations. Remember you can only reserve one park per day in advance, regardless of whether you have park hopper. Also, remember you can make reservations 60 days in advance if you're staying onsite, 30 days in advance if you're not.

Next, select the members of your party for which you wish to book the passes. If you have someone in your family or friends group that has yet to link a ticket, you'll see them listed as shown below. Although you can book passes for different members at different attractions throughout the day, I'll keep it simple and assume you're booking the reservations for your whole party. (If someone decides not to ride, you can always change their reservation to a different attraction later.)

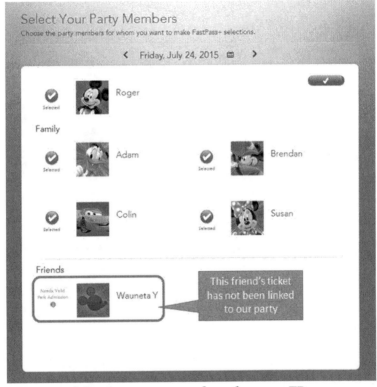

Selecting party members for your FP+

After you select the park and the day, you'll be free to select three attractions at that park. Remember, if you're visiting Hollywood Studios or Epcot you'll be limited to one attraction from Group A and two from Group B. If you're visiting Magic Kingdom or Animal Kingdom, you'll be free to select any three attractions you wish.

Select your attractions and submit them. You'll be presented with four options from which to choose. Your 'Best Match' and three additional options. Pick the times that work best for you and submit. That's it!

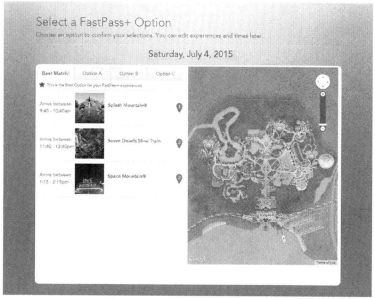

FP+ selection results screen

MODIFYING YOUR FP+ SELECTIONS

So what do you do if none of the four options Disney presents work for you? Perhaps you have a conflicting dining reservation or you're not planning to spend the entire day at that park so the times don't quite work out. What then? Never fear, it's very simple to modify your reservations after you've made them.

Start by selecting the option that most closely matches your schedule for the day, and submit your reservation. Next, on the confirmation screen, click the 'Make Changes' button. You'll be asked if you want to change the time for the selection, or change the reservation to a different attraction. Either way, you'll pick from a new list of times, specify the guests you wish to update, and resubmit. It's that simple!

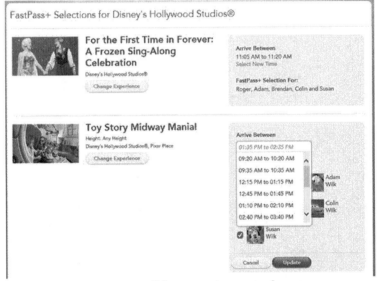

You can modify your times or change the experience completely

If you've already exited the screen, or if you're coming back to update your reservations at a later date, simply return to the 'My Itinerary' screen, select the day, and click the FastPass+ reservation you need to update. You'll follow the same process to update your FP+ as detailed above. Easy, peasy.

UPDATING YOUR FP+ RESERVATIONS WHILE YOU'RE IN THE PARK

Imagine this…. You're smack dab in the middle of a magical day at Magic Kingdom enjoying lunch with Winnie the Pooh and Friends at The Crystal Palace when you realize it's 2:10 p.m.! Your FP+ reservation at Space Mountain expires in five minutes! You'll never make it!

Never fear, everything will be OK. Simply go into the My Disney Experience app on your smart phone and select a new time for your reservation. You will, of course be limited to the times that are still available. It may be that you can't get a reservation at Space Mountain because they've all been booked for the day. This will likely be the case if you've booked the Seven Dwarfs Mine Train in Fantasyland, or if you're at Hollywood Studios and have a reservation for Toy Story Midway Mania. If this is the case, you'll need to pick a new attraction but at least you don't completely lose your third and final FP+ reservation for the day.

WHAT IF YOU'VE MISSED YOUR FP+ RESERVATION?

If you've lost track of time and completely missed your FP+ reservation, things are a bit trickier but it's still not the end of the world. Since you can't change a reservation after it has expired, you'll have to wait until you've used your third and final reservation of the day, or until that reservation has expired. (If you've missed your last one, this will already be the case.)

Since you're only allowed to reserve or update your original three reservations using the My Disney Experience app, from that point forward you'll have to make any new reservations at one of the in-park kiosks. (The locations of the kiosks and convenient maps are located near the end of the previous chapter.) Simply walk up to one of the kiosks and scan your magic band or park ticket. You'll be presented with menus similar to those in the desktop or mobile app. You'll only be presented with a list of attractions that still have passes remaining, so depending on the time of day and the park you're in, your choices may be limited.

The good news is that after you've reserved your new attraction at the kiosk, you can again modify it if necessary from the My Disney Experience app following the instructions in the section above.

That pretty much sums up the process for booking and updating FP+ reservations. It's fairly simple and once you get the hang of it I think you'll find it to be an extremely user-friendly and useful addition to your Walt Disney World vacation.

In the next chapter, I'll talk about all the other cool things you can do with My Disney Experience.

6) ALL THE OTHER THINGS YOU CAN DO WITH MY DISNEY EXPERIENCE

The usefulness of My Disney Experience does not end with the ability to make and update your FastPass+ reservations. In fact, FP+ represents only a small portion of all the cool things you can do with the app.

Since you'll be primarily using the mobile app during your vacation, most of the examples in this section will be from mobile screens. Although the menus and "look and feel" of the desktop and tablet versions are slightly different, the information here should be enough to help you feel comfortable with any version of My Disney Experience. If you do not own a smart phone or tablet, never fear- you can still perform all the tasks detailed below from the desktop version of the app. You just won't have the luxury of using the app to make or update plans while in the parks. After reading this section and doing a bit of exploring on your own, I'm sure you'll agree that My Disney Experience is key to making YOUR Disney experience a magical experience indeed!

I'll begin by explaining the tabs across the top of the mobile app, as they represent the primary functions of the app. There are additional items available if you click the Mouse ears on the upper left-hand side of the screen, but many of those are redundant (or at least similar) to the primary navigation I described in the previous chapter. I'll explain the items unique to that menu after I cover the main items across the top.

Directly below are samples of the tabs you'll find in the current app. I'll explain each in the next several sections.

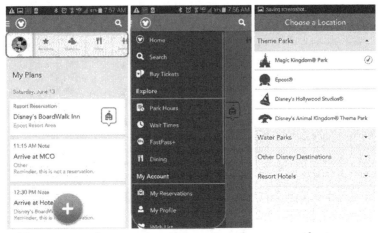

You can navigate using the main tabs across the top, or tap the Mickey to open up the main menu

If you're using the iPad version of My Disney Experience, you'll notice the information is presented in a slightly different manner. There are no tabs across the top of the screen, and the hamburger menu (three little lines at the top left of the screen) opens the primary functionality of the app (similar to tapping the mouse ears at the top left of the mobile app). I'll explain those unique functions at the end of this section, just know that as you move through the sections below, they'll be presented differently, in a slightly different order in the iPad version.

You can 'swipe' to view different parks on the iPad version

MY PLANS

The My Plans tab (the color image of Mickey) shows any and all reservations you've made so far. If you scroll down the list you'll see resort reservations, FP+ reservations, dining reservations, and any 'Plans' you've added for each day of your vacation. If you tap the listed item, you'll see the details for that item. Tap the purple icon on the right (which varies by type of item) and you'll see a really cool map of your destination. You can pinch to zoom in and out so you'll know exactly where you're going when the time comes.

ATTRACTIONS

The next tab is the Attractions tab. In its simplest form, the Attractions tab is merely an alphabetic list of all attractions. You can use the drop-down menu at the bottom to filter the list to any of the four theme parks, the water parks, other Disney destinations such as the

Boardwalk or Downtown Disney, or resort hotels. You'll find this tab to be very useful as you plan your vacation and plot out the things you're going to do each day. It's also very useful as a 'virtual explorer' to learn more about all the things that Disney World has to offer.

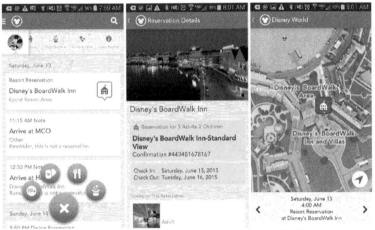

Resort reservation and detail available from the My Plans tab

As with the My Plans tab, and with every tab available in the app, you can tap the attraction listed to find out more about it and also tap the purple icon to see the attraction on a map with the same pinch to zoom options as described in the My Plans section. Attractions running continuously without wait times will all have a 'star' icon. Attractions offering FastPass+ reservations are also labeled as such with a small round "FP+" icon. Each attraction detail page also contains a heart icon that you can tap to add items to your 'wish list' that can be reviewed later.

Attractions tab and details for Soarin'®

Another very useful feature of the Attractions tab are the ride wait time listings. Each attraction is marked with the current wait time which will be very useful to you for example if you're over in Fantasyland at Magic Kingdom and you're wondering if you have time to walk over to Buzz LightYear to ride before lunch. Being able to check ride wait times from anywhere in the park, rather than needing to walk to the attraction or to locate one of the ride wait times boards posted in the parks is a tremendous benefit that will also save you tons of time. Be sure to use it!

Before you leave this tab, there are a couple of other items, both on the bottom menu bar, you should be sure to explore. Tap the little funnel icon next to the park name to bring up tons of ways you can filter the attractions. There are two main tabs listed at the top of the 'filter by' section: Name and Wait Time. I'm not sure why they're listed this way (since they don't really filter anything). They do however allow you to change the way the attractions are sorted. The alphabetic list is useful when you're scrolling through the attraction list looking for details about a specific attraction. Use the Wait Time tab if you want to quickly identify the attractions with the shortest lines. This could help you pack a large number of attractions into the shortest period of time.

Using filters to narrow your list of attractions

You should also check out the extensive list of 'filter by' options that appear when you click the funnel icon. You can filter attractions based on age, height, interests and more. This is especially useful if you're traveling with someone in a wheelchair that may need help getting from the chair to the attraction, or who may not be able to get out of the chair at all. This section allows you to filter the list to only the attractions they can ride, which will save you tons of time throughout your day at Walt Disney World. With height being one of the filters, parents of young children will find this tool to be useful too. You can filter the list down to only the rides your little ones are tall enough to ride which will help you avoid the tears that are sure to flow if you walk all the way across the park only to realize your little one doesn't quite make the cut. There are countless ways you can use the filter function on the Attractions tab, so be sure to explore so you can put the app to work for you.

The last thing you should check out on this tab is the map icon at the very bottom left of the screen. When you tap it, it brings up a super cool interactive map of the selected park, resort, or other Disney destination. From there you can pinch to zoom in and out, or click one of the purple icons to bring up the details for the attraction.

CHARACTERS

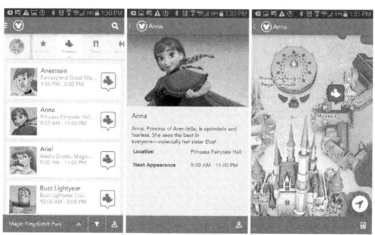

Use the characters tab to find your favorites!

The 'Characters' tab will be very useful if you have little ones (or maybe even you!) who have their heart set on meeting, and getting a picture or autograph with their favorite Disney character. It is only visible when you've tapped to see the details for a location that actually offers character meet and greets.

You can sort this list by character name or location to make it easy to find your favorite princess or Disney pal no matter who it is or where you are. The search results will provide a description of the character, their location, and the times of their next appearance. As with the other tabs, you can also locate the characters by tapping the map icon on the bottom right-hand side of the screen.

DINING

The dining tab (with its cute little knife and fork icon) is a great way to explore all of the different food offerings at Walt Disney World and is an essential tool if you're on the Disney dining plan. It has a similar filter option at the bottom of the screen as in the attractions tab, however this functionality for dining is actually much more useful.

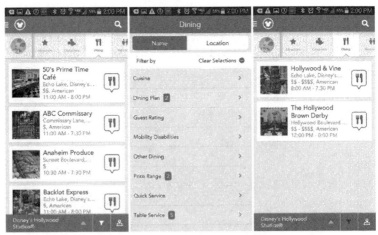

Use multiple filters to find the perfect restaurant

After you've selected your park, hotel, or other Disney destination, you can filter the results by items such as type of cuisine, type of dining plan, guest rating, and price. Another very useful feature for those on the dining plan is the ability to filter the list down to only quick service or table service offerings including several options for each. As with the attractions tab, the dining detail page also contains a heart icon that you can tap to add items to your 'wish list' to be reviewed later.

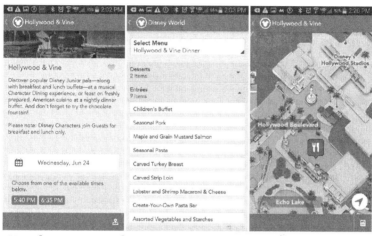

Use the app to make reservations, check menus, and even find the restaurant!

Let's say for example, you're on the dining plan and you still have your table service meal available to use for the day. You certainly don't want to miss out on that! You can filter the list to table service results, and then down to 'character dining' or 'dinner show' offerings for example. It's easy to do, and from there you can make your selection to filter the list, and even make a reservation- all with just a few taps on the screen. Even if you're not on the dining plan, this will be an extremely useful feature as you plan your meals throughout the day.

When you tap to open up the detail for each restaurant, you'll find a brief description of the type of experience you can expect, and a photo so you can get a feel for the atmosphere of the establishment. You are also able to view current breakfast, lunch, and dinner menus for each location including current prices. Finally, you'll find park hours and the location of each restaurant within each park.

The last, and most important of the things you can do in the dining tab is actually make a reservation. Just select a date, and tap the "Find a Table" option on the detail page to see a list of available times for your party. It's great to be able to do all of this in one place without needing to pick up the phone or walk over to the restaurant to see the menu offerings or to find out if there's a table available.

RESTROOMS

Probably the least likely to be used feature of the My Disney Experience app, but most valuable if you really, REALLY need it, is the ability to look up and see a map of any restroom location in any park, hotel, or other Disney destination in all of Walt Disney World. You'll find this tab will be very useful if you have younger children or toddlers just out of diapers who suddenly proclaim, "I gotta go!"

Just select your location to see a list and tap the generic purple men/women restroom icon to see a map to the location. You can also tap the restroom name to see a short description or find out more about it, but really with restrooms (as in real estate) it's all about location, location, location! If you have to 'go' when you're on the go, the Restrooms tab can be a very useful feature.

When you 'gotta go', My Disney Experience will get you there in a hurry

For this tab, the little map pin icon at the bottom right of the screen will be very useful too. You can use it to zoom in on a specific section of the park to quickly find the closest restroom to your current location.

ENTERTAINMENT

The Entertainment tab is where you'll find things like character meet and greets, parades, and shows. It is somewhat redundant to functionality presented in the other tabs, but is a great way to locate and learn more about events that might not be listed in the other categories. Want to learn more about the Main Street Philharmonic? Catch a performance of the Notorious Banjo

Brothers in Magic Kingdom's Frontierland? Check out the show times for the Indiana Jones Epic Stunt Spectacular at Hollywood Studios? Then this is the tab you'll need!

Use multiple filters to select and add attractions to your plans

Everything here works the same as in the other tabs, but this option has a neat feature that allows you to add an item to your plans. Although this is not a true reservation, if you click the Add to My Plans tab presented on the detail page, you'll be able to add this item to your vacation itinerary for the selected date and time. Doing so will keep it neatly organized in your list of things to do so you'll be sure not to miss out. Each Entertainment detail page also contains a heart icon that you can tap to add items to your 'wish list' to save them for later.

EVENTS & TOURS

The Events & Tours tab is a great place to discover all sorts of neat little side items you can add to your Disney vacation. Take an in-depth, 5-hour look at the world's most iconic theme park on the Keys to the Kingdom tour (not coincidentally also the name of my Magic Kingdom theme park guide), Plan a visit for some sprucing up at Main Street U.S.A.'s Harmony Barber Shop, or explore Disney's The Magic Behind Our Steam Trains Tour, all by visiting the Events & Tours tab. Of course as with all the other attractions and tabs, you can click the map icon to help you find your way there.

Use My Disney Experience to find behind the scenes tours

You'll find lots of cool information about many little known tours and activities throughout Walt Disney World, some of which are rarely publicized. Unfortunately, you can't actually book these items through the app at this time, but it's a fun little research project for you to explore as you plan your Disney vacation (or while you're waiting in line at Soarin').

GUEST SERVICES

The Guest Services tab provides details about items such as accessibility services for guests with special needs, the location of ATMs, and even the locations of Automated

External Defibrillators (AEDs) throughout Walt Disney World. You'll also find information about Baby Care Centers, the Car Care Center, Mobile Charging Stations (which you'll need if you're using My Disney Experience frequently in the parks), and even the locations of FastPass+ kiosks (in case you don't have this book with you).

Filtering and sorting options, as well as map viewing functionality is the same here as it is throughout the app.

SHOPPING

Use My Disney Experience to discover your retail nirvana

The final, and most expensive tab of the main tabs listed across the top of the My Disney Experience mobile app is the Shopping tab. Here you can locate any and every place you could possibly think of to shop in Walt Disney World. After you select the location, the results can be listed by name or location within the park, and filtered by categories such as Mickey Ears (who knew?), Pins & Vinylmation (which are pretty much everywhere), Toys & Plush, Art & Collectibles, and even MagicBands.

Amazingly enough (or maybe not so surprising) there are nearly 50 places to shop for gifts and souvenirs in Magic Kingdom alone! Tap each location to see store hours and find out a bit more about the treasures you'll discover there. Oh- and of course there's also the map. Disney wants to be sure you'll have no trouble finding your favorite gift shop!

ADDITIONAL MY DISNEY EXPERIENCE FUNCTIONALITY

Although the main tabs across the top of the app represent the majority of the functionality you'll use on a day-to-day basis during your trip and trip planning, there are still a number of features accessible from the 'Mickey Ears' icon (or hamburger menu) at the top left-hand side of the app screens.

Search: The Search feature listed just below the home link is customizable and can be filter on pretty much everything. This is really just an additional way to search for the information presented in the main tabs. Just below that is the Buy Tickets menu item.

Buy Tickets: This is great functionality that was recently added to the app. You specify the number of days, adult and kid counts, and ticket options, and you'll be presented the price per day as well as the grand total for your ticket purchase. For an in-depth look at Disney ticket options and pricing, as well as how to determine which ticket option is best for your family, please check out my Amazon best-seller: Discover the Magic: The Ultimate Insider's Guide to Walt Disney World, which devotes an entire chapter to Disney ticket information.

EXPLORE

Park Hours: The Park Hours tab shows the hours for all the parks and other Disney destinations such as Disney's Boardwalk and the ESPN Wide World of Sports complex on any given day, and provides a brief overview of each. This is a quick and easy way to see which parks have morning or evening Extra Magic Hours on a given day, and is a great tool to use for your long-term planning and booking your FastPass+ reservations in advance. This section also provides a brief explanation of what Extra Magic Hours are all about.

Use the app to check park hours and wait times (iPad version)

Wait Times: This tab has the exact same functionality as the Attractions tab. The only difference is the default sorting option. Attractions are listed in this tab are sorted by wait time whereas the default for the Attractions tab is sorted alphabetically. As with the Attractions tab, this tab offers several filtering options such as age, height, interests, thrill factor, and disability services to allow you to view only the attractions of interest to you.

FastPass+: This tab is where you go to reserve or update your FP+ reservations, and is essentially everything I covered in chapters 3 and 4 of this book. Since you're way past that point in the book, you're already an expert on this one.

Dining: The Dining tab accessible from the main menu is similar to the dining section I covered earlier. However, in addition to enabling you to search for restaurants by name, location, or type of cuisine, this tab allows you to quickly view the dining reservations you've already made. This will help ensure you do not forget about and miss a reservation you may have made several months prior which would result in a missed reservation penalty, and it's also a quick way to ensure all reservations you've made are correctly linked to your account. If any are missing, you simply enter the confirmation number of the reservation to link it to your account.

MY ACCOUNT

My Reservations: The My Reservations tab is the last tab in the My Disney Experience app that you'll actually use on a regular basis. It provides the opportunity to review at a glance, all reservations, complete with confirmation numbers, which you've made for your upcoming trip. You can also view reservations from previous trips in case you're trying to remember what you did on your last trip to help you prepare for this one. The default View All option lists the reservations by day, grouped by category. The categories are also listed across the top of the screen. They are: Rooms and Packages, Dining Reservations, Tickets and Passes, and FastPass+.

If you tap a reservation you'll see complete details for the reservation including which guests are on the reservation. This is useful to ensure you've included everyone on your FP+ reservations, or if you've split some reservations into two groups, that you've done this correctly. You'd hate to get to the ride entrance and realize you've accidentally booked someone for another attraction instead.

My Profile: This screen provides details of the various account options you've completed as part of your setup. This is also where you can add or change the names of people in your party and where you decide whether or not you want others in your friends list to be able to see your reservations. This is useful if you're traveling with another family or in a large group. It's easier to coordinate who is going to be where, and when, so you can book similar FP+ reservations to ride in a large group. This is also where you can link your tickets and passes to your account, and contains a link to DisneyWorld.com so you can customize your MagicBands (if you're staying onsite).

Last but not least in the My Profile section is the Payment Methods tab that you'll use to add or edit the credit card tied to your account. This is the card that will be charged when you make food or souvenir purchases in the parks and resorts by scanning your MagicBand.

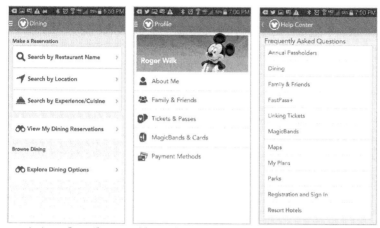

Dining details, profile info, and FAQs round out the app

Wish List: The Wish List tab contains any attractions or activities you've added to your wish list by tapping the little heart icon on an attraction's or activity's detail screen. You can't add new wish list items here, but you can remove them from the list by tapping to get to the detail screen and then tapping the heart to de-select it. You can use this as a way to check off the items in your Wish List as you complete them to make sure your list is empty by the end of your trip.

Notifications: This tab contains any notifications you would have received via email regarding your trip and reservations. This is where you'll be notified that you've successfully linked your tickets, that your MagicBands have shipped, etc.

HELP & SUPPORT

This section of the menu is one you will rarely use. The Help Center selection provides links to frequently asked questions and contains various phone numbers for Disney resort reservations, tickets, etc. There's also a link to the My Disney Experience support number that will come in handy should you have issues with the app.

The Privacy & Legal menu option contains links to terms of use, the privacy policy, and the My Disney Experience terms and conditions. There is also a page that explains how the RF (Radio Frequency) chip works in the MagicBands and how the information is used throughout Walt Disney World.

7) FASTPASS+ TIPS AND TRICKS

As you've probably guessed by now, FastPass+ in its basic form is pretty simple and easy to grasp. You use it to make your ride reservations at Walt Disney World. Having read this book, you now know things go much deeper than that. There are many tricks and tips you can utilize to get more from the system, and to be ahead of the other 'basic' users. Here are some tricks and tips to help you get more out of Disney's FastPass+ system to help you make the most of your Disney vacation.

- Due to the fact that you can't obtain more FassPass+'s until after you've used your initial three, it's best to get them earlier in the day when reserving them in advance with the My Disney Experience app. It increases the chances that there will be passes left for the top attractions when you reserve your 'add on' passes later in the day at the park kiosks.

- That being said, if you plan to arrive at a park when it opens, do not bother making your FastPass+ reservations for the first couple of hours of the day. With very few exceptions (most notably Toy Story Midway Mania at Hollywood Studios and Seven Dwarfs Mine Train at Magic Kingdom), chances are the wait times early in the day will not warrant the use of one of your precious three reservations. You'll be better off waiting in the standby lines during this time and starting your FastPass+ reservations when the park begins to get more crowded (usually around 11:00 a.m.).

- The FastPass+ attractions at Epcot and Hollywood Studios are in groups. Because of this, you won't be able to pick any three attractions in those two parks. You'll need to pick from an attraction in each group so you won't necessarily get to select all of your favorites.

- Use the My Disney Experience app to check out the wait times for the most popular attractions in advance. That may help you decide which to select as you choose your FastPass+ attractions.

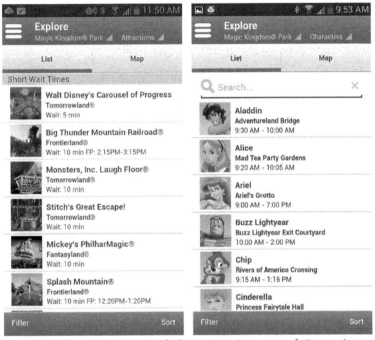

Check wait times and character 'Meet and Greets' with the My Disney Experience app

- Reserve your attractions as soon as you get your tickets, or as soon as you're eligible if you purchase your tickets far in advance. Remember- 30 days in advance if you're staying off of Disney property, and 60 days in advance if you're staying at a Disney resort. You'll get the best times that way, with the most flexibility in your planning, plus you can always change your reservations if your plans change.

- The My Disney Experience app will suggest times for you, but don't feel like you are required to take the suggestions. You have the freedom to choose other attractions and times.

- When the app displays the four options from which to choose, make sure you pick the one that has the three attractions you've requested. By the time you get to the 3rd or 4th choice, there may be attractions listed other than the original three you selected.

- Don't worry if one of the attraction times conflicts with your other plans. Select the option for all three that works best, then go back and change the time on the attraction that doesn't work for you.

- Be careful when choosing your selections that you select all members of your party (if that's your intent). You don't want to leave anyone behind in the standby line because you forgot to include them while making the reservations

- When looking for FP+ kiosks in the parks to add new reservations or change an existing one, look for the ones near the back of the parks or off the beaten path. They'll be less likely to have a big crowd around waiting to use the kiosks

- When you get to the kiosks don't be afraid to ask the Disney cast member for assistance. They're there to help! The technology is new to all of us and confusing at times. Don't worry- you're not dumb!

- If you review the FastPass+ ratings section for each of the parks, you'll notice that very few shows or meet and greets are worthy of taking up one of your FP+ reservations. However if you check the My Disney Experience app and find that one of the meet and greets is in extremely high demand (as indicated by the long wait times) you may find it worth your while if it's on your Disney bucket list. For example, if your little princess is dying to meet Anna and Elsa, this may be worthy of one of your FP+ reservations.

- If you're staying offsite and are jealous of all the vacationers with those spiffy MagicBands, never fear- they're available for purchase in the parks. Wearing these beauties on your wrist is much more convenient than needing to pull out your ticket to scan it at each of the park entrances and FP+ return entrances.

- Remember- you can't get additional FastPass+ reservations until you use up your initial three (or the last one has expired). If you choose to reserve premium seating for one of the evening spectaculars such as Wishes, IllumiNations, or Fantasmic, you'll be limited to three that day. This is because you can't get your 4th until the show ends and the park will likely be closing afterward, or at the very least the FP+ reservations will be gone.

8) LET THE MAGIC (AND MEMORIES) BEGIN!

Let the memories begin!

Whew! That was a lot to digest, I know. Who knew that so much planning and prep work went into a Disney vacation? Now you're miles ahead of those that decided to just 'wing it' (or maybe they just didn't know any better) and head to the parks without any planning, FastPass+ reservations, or direction.

If you started reading this book with little to no knowledge of FastPass+, you now know everything you need to know to use it to your advantage. I've provided a bit of history to help you understand how we made it to where we are today, and I've given you plenty of tips and strategies to help you make the most of Disney's very effective and efficient reservation system.

I've provided a complete walk-through of My Disney Experience and how you'll use it to make and update your FP+ and other Disney reservations. You're now an expert in all the other functionality the app provides as well. From monitoring attraction wait times before your trip to plot and plan your experience, to knowing how to find your favorite Disney characters in the parks, to using the Wish List functionality of the app to help you keep track of all the wonderful things that you hope to make part of your Disney experience, My Disney Experience was designed to make **your** Disney experience the best that it can be.

Have a magical day!

You should now have the knowledge and confidence to embark on the most magical Disney vacation ever! Enjoy your trip- and follow me on Twitter (@Disney4Families) or on Facebook at: www.facebook.com/DisneyVacations4Families so you can let me know how it goes. Have a magical day!

WAIT- There's one more thing...

If you've enjoyed this book, I hope you'll share it with family & friends. I would love it if you would **please** visit the Amazon book page. It just takes a minute. If you scroll down the page and click the **Write a Customer Review** button it will help me share the knowledge and strategies outlined in this book with others. Take a minute to "Like" my Disney Facebook page and follow me on Twitter (@Disney4Families). With so many changes constantly occurring at Disney, it's guaranteed that something will be different a few months down the road. I'll post many park updates on Facebook and Twitter, so that's the best way to keep in touch. This is also where I'll announce new books, updates, book sales and FREE BOOK promotions.

Thanks so much for reading- Have a Magical Day!

Roger

ALSO BY ROGER WILK...

Discover the Magic: The Ultimate Insider's Guide to Walt Disney World

The all new for 2015 Ultimate Walt Disney World theme park guide packed with vacation planning and travel tips for Magic Kingdom, Epcot, Hollywood Studios, Animal Kingdom- and even Disney's awesome water parks: Typhoon Lagoon and Blizzard Beach! Discover Disney resorts like never before. Discover the Magic will guide you every step of the way as you prepare to embark on the trip of a lifetime- an adventure like no other. A magical vacation to Walt Disney World!
Discover the Magic today!!!

Disney Tips & Secrets: Unlocking the Magic of a Walt Disney World Vacation

Experience a magical Disney vacation- updated and EXPANDED with 240 tips and secrets to save time and MONEY while taking the stress out of your Disney vacation. Whether you're going to The Magic Kingdom, Animal Kingdom, Hollywood Studios, or Epcot, we've got you covered! Discover hidden paths and a secret exit from The Magic Kingdom. Beat the crowds as you head for the monorail back to the parking lots or your hotel. Learn the secrets to vacation photos and **so much more!**
Get Disney Tips & Secrets today!!!

Keys to the Kingdom: Your Complete Guide to Walt Disney World's Magic Kingdom Theme Park

Prepare to experience the crown jewel of Disney parks. Prepare to be enchanted by the **Magic Kingdom!** In **Keys to the Kingdom** you'll find everything you need to make the most of your Disney vacation including detailed maps, ride guides, dining guides, and **more!** You'll also get complete guides to Magic Kingdom's awesome shows & parades. Neatly organized and supported by nearly 70 photos, maps, and charts, the **Keys to the Kingdom** are ready to unlock the magic of **your** Disney vacation!

Disney Christmas Magic: The Ultimate Insider's Guide to Spending the Holidays at Walt Disney World

Experience the happiest place on Earth during the most magical season on Earth- the Christmas holiday season! Learn all about the special holiday events at Walt Disney World like Mickey's Very Merry Christmas Party at Magic Kingdom, Epcot's Candlelight Processional, and the Osborne Family Spectacle of Dancing Lights at Hollywood Studios. All this and more awaits!
Discover Disney Christmas Magic today!!!

Made in the USA
San Bernardino, CA
01 October 2015